Home Theater Systems

Jim Stephens

Published by RWG Publishing, 2021.

HOME THEATER SYSTEMS

First edition. June 18, 2021.

Written by Jim Stephens.

Also by Jim Stephens

Kindle Publishing Made Easy: Autopilot Cash With Amazon Kindle!
Million-Dollar Secrets of the Amazon Associates: How They Make Money
From the Biggest Online Shopping Mall
Self-Publishing Made Easy: The Easy Way to Self-publish Your Own Books!
Scam Busters: How to Avoid the Most Popular Scams of Today!
Affiliate Marketing and Blogging
The Quick and Easy Guide of Diamonds
Government Information
Hiking and Camping
Home Theater Systems

Table of Contents

Basic Components for a Home Theater

Numerous individuals never trouble investigating buying a home performance center through sheer dread of the choices that may should be made all the while. Numerous among these aren't even certain of precisely what parts are remembered for a home theater or which ones are required to make a viable and engaging home theater. Thus, numerous individuals just try not to go through the way toward taking a gander at their choices with regards to these great frameworks available today significantly less at any point trouble really buying one.

In the event that you are one of the numerous who has encountered some level of disarray with regards to the individual parts and pieces that are remembered for a home theater framework and what they do, ideally you will acquire a superior agreement whenever you've completed the process of perusing. The primary thing to comprehend is that there are differing degrees with regards to home theaters. The accompanying parts are the makings of an essential home auditorium that will give phenomenal usefulness. They are not anyway comprehensive of each conceivable piece or part that could make up a home theater framework.

Off to the fundamentals, the principal thing you'll require while making a home venue for your family to appreciate is a TV. It may appear to be excessively clear to a few yet I presently can't seem to discover a crate unit that incorporates a TV—primarily in light of the fact that the decision of screen is for some the most close to home part of choosing a home theater. There are basically three decisions in the present TV market: front projector, back projector, and plasma. There are varieties inside every one of these and the costs fall anyplace from unobtrusive to very expensive. This is the segment that most home theater proprietors invest the most energy examining and it influences the sorts of parts that will be best later on in footing of things, for example, superior quality and different decisions you can make.

A beneficiary is another significant segment. You will presumably have a DVD player or recorder or something to that affect as a component of your framework; you may have a Tivo and link box or satellite and will most likely have speakers or some likeness thereof for your framework. The recipient is the

1

case you plug them all into—it gets the entirety of this information sources and associates it as it were. This is a definitive traffic chief with regards to your home theater and I propose you spend a decent bit of your home venue spending ensuring that this is a decent quality part.

Speakers are the place where your sound will stream. Probably the best thing to me about a home auditorium is the capacity to encounter encompass sound basically the same as what I experience in theaters while being able to rest or cuddle under covers (which essentially can't be accomplished in a theater). Speakers come in all shapes and measures and are likewise very close to home for certain customers while compromise for other people. You can buy these are essential for a pack to make the determination interaction simpler.

At last, you have your DVD player or recorder. On the off chance that superior quality is essential to you, you currently have that alternative. In the event that your TV isn't HD prepared or competent, I'd pass and go for a more seasoned (more affordable) model of DVD player until something more cutting-edge is called for. These things are an incredible beginning for any home theater and you can construct, grow, and overhaul after some time for a far better framework. Appreciate!

Box Kit Home Theaters

We face a daily reality such that accommodation is progressively filling popular. Consequently many home theater purchasers expect comfort with regards to the buy and set up of their home theater frameworks. It's implied that there are a wide range of purchasers on the planet and surprisingly in issue of comfort organic market have not arisen to make a one size fits all general public. We as a whole need comparable things from multiple points of view yet we actually need self-sufficiency and choices from which to pick.

The requests of a general public that likes the simplicity of purchasing prepackaged products have arrived at such a point anyway that bundles are regular spot in everything from prepackaged meals to prepackaged home theater frameworks. On one level these sorts of prepackaged theater frameworks give a lot of accommodation to customers. Among those advantages is the capacity to know the expense of the whole framework in advance. This is really a little advantage when contrasted with a portion of different advantages that shoppers who buy these frameworks experience.

Similarity

Customers who buy these pre bundled home theater frameworks know when they purchase the framework that each part will work related to different parts in the framework. There are no exclusive issues to stress over, the parts have been made and planned with the purpose of functioning admirably together as well as of supplementing each other simultaneously. All pieces cooperate for most extreme quality and productivity—at the cost.

Cost

A large portion of these boxed frameworks will cost not as much as buying comparable individual segments. For some, this by itself is a sufficient motivation to buy a case pack. This is really notwithstanding the accommodation of knowing the cost for the whole bundle early. There is a wide assortment of parts and segments available and you can discover numerous pieces in each value range, it is regularly befuddling when looking at costs since it is frequently hard to comprehend subtleties of value basically by contrasting boxes.

Information

With regards to the prepackaged box packs, you can really see and hear them in real life as a piece of the opening. This implies that you realize how the framework will sound when cooperating instead of hearing a mixed bag of pieces and segments while staying uncertain of how they truly work exclusively. There is a great deal to be said about the capacity to take a stab at something before you get it. Prepackaged home theater frameworks permit shoppers to do exactly that.

Establishment

This for some is presumably the most compelling motivation to go with the prepackaged unit as opposed to an immense arrangement of individual part—simplicity of establishment. Most, if not all, of the prepackaged packs are easy to introduce, which takes out the requirement for proficient establishment and takes a lot of issue out of the establishment interaction.

The prepackaged frameworks are not in any case, the kind of frameworks you will need to buy in the event that you expect to construct a superior framework over the long haul as they are not effectively upgradeable and most obvious aficionados are frequently disillusioned with the nature of the speakers and sounds that accompany these frameworks. In any case in the event that you have restricted space and restricted assets, these frameworks are regularly an incredible spot to begin with regards to a home theater. You can generally give it to your kids in the event that you choose to overhaul later.

Building a Great Home Theater

It very well may be exceptionally simple to burn through huge number of dollars assembling a definitive home auditorium experience for you and your family and in the event that you utilize your home venue consistently and have the cash to save you may discover certainly worth the speculation. Nonetheless, you can likewise fabricate a phenomenal home auditorium for altogether less cash in the event that you will invest a lot of energy into tracking down the correct parts at the correct cost for your framework. All that comes down to issue of inclination and accessible assets when constructing any kind of home theater.

The reality of the situation is that the majority of us can't bear to spend in excess of 10,000 dollars making the home performance center we had always wanted. A large number of us should genuinely spending admirably to put several thousand dollars on our home theaters. Fortunately for two or three thousand dollars you can make a really extraordinary home theater on the off chance that you get your work done and put your cash carefully in segments for your home theater framework.

My first suggestion when fabricating a decent quality home performance center is to get each piece in turn as opposed to building everything simultaneously. This permits you to continually redesign your framework without breaking the spending at the same time. It likewise permits you an opportunity to set something aside for better quality pieces inside your framework instead of endeavoring to make a win or bust buy. One thing to recall when buying pieces separately is to ensure that they are on the whole viable (this is particularly significant with speakers, which I suggest buying all together at whatever point conceivable).

The TV is the principal thing you should buy when constructing your home auditorium as nearly everything in your home venue will revolve around your TV. Superior quality TVs are getting increasingly normal and give better quality than numerous different TVs you will discover available. In the event that you have the methods with which to buy this kind of TV I strongly suggest that you do as such. When you have your TV you can start buying different segments to finish your framework.

The following part I suggest is a collector or enhancer. This is the piece that unites any remaining segments. Without a good beneficiary it is essentially difficult to have a respectable home theater. The beneficiary goes about as a kind of conductor for the sound and image of your home theater. This is a piece of hardware that ought not be held back on with regards to quality, as you will totally miss a significant piece of the 'theater' experience without it.

Next are the speakers. Speakers are likewise vital to the 'theater' experience of your home theater. The speakers are what give that 'film quality' sound that is so critical to most fans and what will make your framework the jealousy of the area. I strongly suggest buying speakers as a set to guarantee similarity.

At last, the DVD player or recorder balances the framework. It is dependent upon you and your inclinations whether you wish to put resources into a high dollar (right now) superior quality DVD player. In the event that you have HD TV and plan to buy HD circles for your motion pictures then this is the best approach. Else it is a finished misuse of cash as I would see it until the remainder of your framework ascends to meet the innovation. The beneficial thing about buying each segment in turn is that you can continually run after overhauling your framework to meet rising innovation.

Building a Home Theater on a Tight spending plan

Americans will in general invest a ton of energy before our TVs. Regardless of whether we are film addicts with numerous enrollments to Internet film rental organizations or are not kidding addicts to everything reality on TV we are dependent on our amusement. Since we invest such a lot of energy watching our TVs it bodes well that we cause a sizeable interest in our home performance center to get the most ideal quality picture and sound from our frameworks.

We don't, anyway live in a one size fits all world, which has lead to a decent arrangement of solid contest inside media outlets just as the gadgets business. This is amazing information for purchasers that should live inside the requirements of their financial plans. As rivalry arises alongside more current advances we see a descending pattern in the costs of existing innovation. The genuine stunt anyway is to be content with a year ago's innovation today and you could really save thousands on your home theater.

In the event that you are in any event, willing to go a stage back the extent that innovation, trust me it isn't advancing all that recognizably quick with regards to home theaters, you can in any case get an incredible home venue on Ebay or even in your neighborhood paper that is of superb quality for a negligible part of the expense you would have paid for the framework had you bought it spic and span. In the event that you are only thrifty or are going through a spending starvation you should find that there are some remarkable choices accessible through recycled home theaters.

In the event that you resemble many (and there is literally nothing amiss with this) who don't care for buying utilized things out of the blue, the most widely recognized being an absence of a guarantee, at that point it bodes well not to think about this specific choice. Choosing this alternative anyway doesn't leave you without choices using any and all means. Maybe my number one choice is to assemble your own home auditorium each piece in turn. You may be astounded to track down that in the end you have a better framework than the greater part of those you will discover available today.

Life is a progression of decisions and that interaction doesn't end at all when you are picking the correct home auditorium for your home and needs. Sadly neither does the way that we regularly should live inside spending limitations that we don't appreciate close to however much we appreciate the possibility of Dolby Digital Surround Sound or Bose speakers. Fortunately on the off chance that you look and take as much time as is needed by looking at and contrasting your preferences in numerous frameworks you will have become an educated buyer. This is simply the best blessing you can give when looking.

Look at costs, ask, deal, and deal. Check whether stores will coordinate with the costs of different stores or toss in gifts to contend. You ought to likewise recollect that except if you have the hardware and abilities important for the establishment of your home theater almost certainly, you should pay for that too. A retailer that will toss in free establishment may be a deal worth giving somewhat more idea.

Eventually, the objective is to get the most ideal home auditorium for your home for minimal measure of cash conceivable. By finding out about your alternatives you will know when you leave the store whether you got a decent arrangement on the home theater you purchased. There can't be sufficient said about the information you will acquire about home venues through this interaction or what you will find out about the cost of things contrasted with their worth. All the more critically you could actually become familiar with the genuine value we regularly pay basically to go with a name that we know. You can save a lot of cash by taking a risk on arising organizations however do your examination clench hand and find out however much about the organization as could reasonably be expected before you give them your well deserved cash.

Purchasing a Home Theater Within your Means

When arranging and buying a home theater you may track down that notwithstanding a wide scope of decisions you are additionally confronted with a limit and huge swath of valuing choices for your home theater needs. Regardless of whether you are looking for a framework that is just a decent methods for watching your number one game on some random Sunday or you are wanting to track down a home theater framework that will be the jealousy of the neighborhood there are numerous frameworks accessible inside many spending ranges that will achieve both of those objectives on the off chance that you cautiously plan the framework you will at last buy.

You ought to build up a spending plan prior to going out to shop for your home theater framework and purchase a framework that suits both the necessities you wish to have filled and your methods with which to pay. Fortunately there are some home auditorium bundles that will suit most spending plans; even the most impenetrable and you can generally track down the one framework you like and watch near check whether it goes at a bargain.

The fact is that there truly are a wide range of home theater frameworks available and they shift enormously in value, quality, and degree. Be certain you know precisely the thing you are getting when your buy a home theater framework, particularly in the event that you are getting one of the many home auditorium in a container units that are available today. You may not be getting all that you trust you are getting and it pays to understand what you need concerning what you presently have.

Normal parts you will discover in a home theater framework pack incorporate the accompanying: a recipient, speakers, and a DVD or DVR. Most packs right now available do exclude TVs and a few units being promoted as home auditorium units are only boxes of speakers. This is the reason you need to ensure that you read cautiously and know precisely what is remembered for the 'unit' you are paying for.

In the event that you need another TV all together for your home auditorium to merit anything to you that may be the beginning stage for your home theater framework whereupon you can assemble later. Assuming you have a fair TV that is HD prepared, you are set up to begin looking for a magnificent HD home theater. In the event that your TV isn't HD prepared, it would be a misuse of cash to make the interest in HD gear at the present swelled costs that won't be of prompt use to you. Assuming HD is significant, you should start by buying a HD TV and not form your home auditorium until you have that vital part set up.

Then again, if HD isn't imperative to you right now or you would like to stand by until lower costs win, it is a dependable choice to feel free to buy a home auditorium that has the best innovation you are equipped for using right now. You can really get very great arrangements on what is viewed as the previous innovation (which can be only that new in the present gadgets market) and for some, that is certainly the best approach when purchasing a home theater framework. You can defeat the previous innovation for a negligible part of the expense of many lower quality things that are available today.

The greatest thing to recall when contrasting highlights is with realize what is imperative to you in a home theater framework and purchase with that information. It doesn't bode well to make this kind of speculation in the event that you will find that you can't live with the restrictions of your innovation a half year from now. Consequently, no one but you can choose what is and is anything but a satisfactory cost for you to pay for your home theater framework just as what level of innovation for which you will settle.

Purchasing Home Theater Systems Online

In this day and age a considerable lot of us discover the comfort of web based shopping to be best in class. This is particularly obvious at specific seasons and with specific things. There are still a few things that should be attempted before they are bought. This anyway doesn't imply that you can't appreciate the wide assortment of evaluating choices that are accessible on the web on the off chance that you don't care for the cost of your top picks in the store. One of these things that should be seen (and heard) to have a legitimate thought of its real worth to you is a home theater framework.

You need to visit nearby stores and contrast the items available and each other. You need to hear these frameworks and view these frameworks to decide if you figure they will give the quality you are looking for your home theater framework. Review the frameworks that are sold as a feature of sets additionally permits you to have a smart thought of what ought to be remembered for your normal home theater on the off chance that you choose to buy the segments separately, which I strongly suggest, instead of as one complete pack.

Fortunately whenever you have limited your determinations and have a smart thought of what neighborhood retailers are charging for similar things you can start searching for deals on the web. The issue numerous individuals run over is discovering new brands or frameworks online at stunningly better costs. While this may not seem like a very remarkable issue on one hand, you are never quite certain of who you are managing on the web and not all sellers are trustworthy similarly as all items are not made similarly. There are times in life when you are genuinely getting what you are paying for with regards to deal chasing.

On the off chance that something on the web appears to be unrealistic, this is by and large a sign to pass. In any case, in the event that you can discover similar deals online to a similar item you've found in stores it could merit buying gave you are going through a protected and trustworthy vendor. When shopping on the web for home theater gear, frameworks, or segments you ought to consistently make wellbeing your main goal. On the off chance that you believe you are being requested an excessive amount of individual data it very well might be a smart thought to pass. In the event that you are not sure the site is secure it's a shrewd arrangement to pass, and above all in the event that you have any inquiries, questions, or concerns it is a decent arrangement to pass as opposed to follow through on a more extreme cost later than you had proposed.

The Internet has done a lot to connect the holes all throughout the planet and keeping in mind that it has made numerous things considerably more helpful and pleasant it has likewise made it workable for the deceitful to have an additional battleground among us. Be cautious when giving out data on the web, particularly close to home and monetary data, as you never truly realize who is on the opposite finish of that data. It is not necessarily the case that you shouldn't lead business online just to urge you to go through notable organizations and study audits of organizations and items prior to going with those you're not excessively acquainted with. This can save a lot of time, cash, and bother later on. It does not merit gambling fraud to save a couple of dollars.

Basic Home Theater Mistakes to Avoid

A home venue is no little venture, especially on the off chance that you are going for a decent quality home theater. In light of that there are numerous slip-ups that individuals make en route with regards to their home theaters. What you need to do is gain from the errors of others instead of damning yourself to rehash those that have been made so often previously. Beneath you will discover data on the absolute regularly committed errors with regards to making an extraordinary home performance center for you and your family.

Windows

I'm not talking Microsoft all things considered. One thing that is an executioner for your home performance center is a room brimming with windows. Around evening time, each vehicle passing by will demonstrate diverting and during the day little can be appreciated on your TV from the daylight pouring in. Indeed, even ordinary drapes permit some level of light into the room, which will give a diverting glare on you TV screen. In the event that you have no austere rooms in your home you will at any rate need to introduce some substantial power outage curtains or blinds to forestall the glare and interruption that windows give.

Modest Speakers

Sound is perhaps the main factors in emulating a performance center quality film seeing experience. In the event that you have modest speakers you won't get the nature of sound that you will require to accomplish that experience. The initial five or ten minutes of the film Top Gun gives extraordinary compared to other sound tests I've at any point seen. Get a duplicate of the DVD and take it with you to the stores, think about speakers utilizing that DVD and go with the set that gives the best nature of sound. It's a decent litmus test and you will be happy you did in the event that you at any point tune in to a most loved film on a companions second rate speakers.

Helpless Installation

It looks bad to put a large number of dollars in a home theater framework just to bring it home and make a terrible display of introducing it since you would not like to jump on the additional 200 dollars for establishment. Ill-advised establishment of your home venue will bring about substantially less quality than you paid for, which makes a decent quality framework a total misuse of cash. Follow through on the cost now for proficient establishment in the event that you have any questions whatsoever about your capacity to appropriately introduce your framework.

Not Reading Directions

Then again in the event that you choose to do your own establishment the main issue is the aftereffect of not perusing the guidelines for establishment as well as the activity of your home theater. We may feel that we are instinctive essentially yet now and again it assists with having a guide to follow. Directions for establishment and working manuals are our guides and perusing them first won't just save a lot of time yet in addition increment your satisfaction in your home theater.

Keeping away from these normal missteps can come route towards assisting you with getting the most conceivable happiness from your home theater. It's stunning the amount of a distinction easily overlooked details can make en route. Best of luck with the determination, buy, and establishment of your home theater. I trust you appreciate numerous superb long periods of film, TV, and game watching on your new framework.

Basic Television Types for Home Theaters

While choosing parts for your home theater you will go to a point in time when you should settle on which type and size of TV you will require for the most ideal review insight. There are numerous kinds of TVs available today and innovation is continually advancing and arising to bring fresher, greater, and better TVs to a market that one would believe is as of now immersed.

Fortunately the actual idea of this market makes previous days forefront innovation the present deal of the day. The actual quickness of new innovation in the gadgets business works for purchasers by driving costs down rather rapidly. Nothing is altogether too far for the normal customer for excessively awfully long. Hence you can bear to be genuinely particular while picking segments for your home theater. This particularity just so ends up reaching out to TVs sets too.

There are essentially three kinds of TVs consuming the home auditorium market today. Those kinds of TVs incorporate the accompanying: plasma, back task, or front projection TV. Each of these enjoy unmistakable benefits and inconveniences with regards to home theater.

Plasma Televisions

These TVs frequently give the best quality with regards to picture. Their plans make them ideal for watching films that are organized for wide screen survey and they have a lot bigger review territory than customary TVs and they additionally arrive in a wide assortment of sizes to adjust to numerous kinds of home theater needs. The single biggest issue with these sorts of TVs is the value, which can be very restrictive, especially as you think about the bigger measured TVs.

Back Projection Televisions

Back projection TVs offer a lot of value at a much lower cost than plasma TVs. With these kinds of TVs the picture is anticipated and reflected from the rear of the TV. One of the significant burdens for back projections TVs is the way that they are very sizable to house the segments essential for a decent quality picture onscreen. Another unmistakable hindrance is the way that there is a lot of contest that changes in quality and you truly need to examine the different TVs prior to choosing any one specifically.

Other striking downsides to raise projection TVs are the realities that the lighting in the room influences the nature of the image onscreen and you have a thin review range. Something else, the minimal expense included is an immense reward to numerous and makes the acquisition of this kind of TV (especially for a home theater) the most ideal decision. It generally boils down to a matter of inclination.

Front Projectors

These are not by and large TVs in the conventional feeling of the word however they function admirably for this specific reason and are ideal answers for some home theaters. The innovation for this kind of survey medium has additionally advanced throughout the most recent couple of years. Gone are the times of large cumbersome boxes that sat on the floor of your family room and that nobody could stroll before without genuinely mutilating the TV see. The present front projectors are mounted on the roof and give a decent nature of picture rather you are utilizing a screen that is intended to expand the nature of the image or simply projecting onto a clear divider.

As I referenced before there is no all inclusive correct with regards to choosing the best TV for your home theater. What you should give cautious consideration to is which screen or which see you like best. Which sort of TV will offer you the most value for your home theater money? You ought to likewise ask yourself which level of value can you and can you not live without? These are significant inquiries that should help you thin down your quest for a TV for your home theater.

Contrast Home Theater with Movie Going

Numerous individuals avoid buying a home venue because of a paranoid fear of the extraordinary expenses associated with doing as such. I suggest that you put genuine pen and paper to those suppositions rather then simply expecting it is excessively expensive for your restricted financial plan. The reality of the situation, when contrasted and the expenses of going out to watch a film you may find that you will invest less cash in no energy by watching motion pictures at home instead of paying for the 'film going' experience.

You should give cautious consideration to how much cash you go through every month going to the theater. Remember incorporating any expenses associated with employing sitters, going out to supper (a great many people don't do McDonald's previously or subsequent to going to theaters), snack bar buys in those figures. Regardless of whether you go to the performance center once per week as a team or as family the expenses can truly add up. On the off chance that you visit the performance center less or have a more modest family those expenses may be less however you could likewise truly raise those costs by going all the more frequently or having a bigger family.

The significant thing to recall when estimating a home theater framework is the worth it will bring to you and your family. On the off chance that this will unite the family at home a few evenings every week it is definitely worth the interest as I would see it. On the off chance that it will keep the youngsters in your home and off the roads toward the end of the week it is worth much more. A home performance center is an interest in the pleasure in your home for everybody included and numerous families track down that this is an extraordinary method to appreciate a night at home. It's likewise an extraordinary method to guarantee super—Super Bowl gatherings will be occurring in your home instead of the homes of others (it's a little cost to pay when it's all said and done).

In light of this you can purchase units for anyplace somewhere in the range of $200 and $2,000 (and upwards, however in the event that you will spend more than $2,000 I truly suggest building your own home theater). Box frameworks are somewhat simple to discover in nearby and mass-market retailers and are fairly easy to introduce (in any event, for the unenlightened). These frameworks may not give the most ideal framework yet for the individuals who have huge spending concerns they are an incredible spot to begin and you can get some truly extraordinary frameworks in the event that you are able to genuinely search around and look at the changed quality between brands just as which extravagant accessories you require and which you can live without.

When you settle on the choice to purchase a home auditorium the best thing to do is look at what is accessible. You should then exploit the incredible rivalry available today via looking for the most highlights at the least cost. You could very well be stunned and flabbergasted at the incredible deals that you can discover, particularly soon after the huge buyer exhibition show every January.

You should consolidate the home theater and great film insight in your home with an enrollment to Netflix, Blockbuster, or some other home conveyance DVD framework and you can have frozen pizza, microwave popcorn, and every one of the pads to take cover behind you can request in the solace of your home at a negligible part of the cost of going to the auditorium once per week.

Looking at Prices can Bring Sweet Bargains

Perhaps the most troublesome things for some individuals to do when strolling into a hardware store is as a rule to remain on spending plan. There are such countless chimes, whistles, and just wonderful contraptions available today that it is difficult to go into the store determined to go through a specific measure of cash and staying with that expectation. This being said it is feasible to deal shop and get the most ideal can hope for your cash with regards to buying a great home theater framework in the event that you will do the required legwork.

Genuinely there are a few stages included and it regularly requires numerous outings to different stores or various calls in any event throughout about seven days on schedule. The justification the entirety of this is that it could in a real sense save you many dollars with regards to building your home theater or in any event, when purchasing a prepackaged framework and will at any rate have you equipped with the essential information to get a decent cost on the framework you pick.

A decent home auditorium is a sizeable speculation and not one that ought to be trifled with. While a decent framework should most recent quite a long while, you would truly prefer not to go through more cash than you need to purchase the framework on the off chance that you can keep away from it without any problem. Numerous individuals purchase these frameworks without really thinking or settle on the choice to get one at that point feel they should cause the buy before they to have the opportunity to either work themselves out of it or some other issue comes up, which forestalls the little cushioning in the spending that a home venue will eliminate.

The initial phase in my terrific arrangement for getting a good deal on a home performance center is to look at the neighborhood stores. There are a couple of purposes behind this. As a matter of first importance you have the chance to truly look at the frameworks you are thinking about and contrast them and each other with respect to both quality and the highlights you are looking for. Second, it allows you an opportunity to see the costs and determination that are accessible on the nearby level. Track the costs on the frameworks you like and contrast them with the costs on something similar or comparative frameworks in different stores.

You should then return home and sign on to the Internet. Looking at costs online can regularly introduce some stunning deals. When you track down the most reduced value, make a documentation of the site and print off the data including the cost. When you have paper close by, it's an ideal opportunity to do somewhat more legwork in and out of town. Go to your neighborhood stores with the cost and check whether they will match or beat the value you found on the web. While as a rule you will discover stores that will coordinate yet not beat the costs on the web. Notwithstanding, there are events when the store will toss in a pleasant advantage, for example, a free DVD for your new framework or something along the line as well as coordinating with the value you found on the web.

Basically looking at costs on the web and tracking down the least conceivable cost can frequently mean the distinction in a framework being inside your spending stipend or outside of your recompense. Best case scenario, it can make a home auditorium inside your span to say the least it is very conceivable that you will set aside cash over the nearby store cost by shopping on the web (regardless of whether your neighborhood stores will not match the value you can regularly discover lower costs online with free transportation).

Make your Personal Home Theater

We frequently invest a lot of energy considering the different segments of our home theater frameworks yet seldom really think about to how the style of the room influences our capacity to make the most of our home theaters and motion pictures without the additional interruption of the dividers in the room or other adorning highlights. To get some good thoughts, go to the specialists with regards to planning the most ideal survey encounters. Require a night out at the films and look at the manner in which the room is enriched before the film starts and focus during the film to the things that divert you most.

Theaters rake in tons of cash by making an encounter more than for the basic appearance of films. The primary thing you will likely notification is that most venues don't permit outside light into the room. In actuality, most performance centers have next to no in the method of counterfeit light all things considered. You may detect some divider sconces and some running lights (that can be lit up or diminished) at the edges yet infrequently will you notice any overhead lighting turned on even before the motion pictures play. Hence, storm cellars or inside rooms without any windows are the most ideal decisions with regards to choosing the area for your home theater. On the off chance that that isn't accessible make certain to attempt to discover power outage draperies or curtains for your windows to keep the most conceivable daylight out.

The tones they decided for the dividers and the kinds of lighting they are utilizing are painstakingly chosen to improve that experience. I'm certain you will track down that most venues utilize more obscure shadings for their dividers. Many use texture to line the dividers so gleaming paint doesn't mirror the light from the screen. In your home you can decide on finished paints or mattes to stay away from expected reflections. You ought to likewise ensure that you're not utilizing gleaming floor surfaces that may likewise mirror the light back onto the screen. Hence cover settles on a decent ground surface decision for your home theater.

Something else you will need to ensure that your home venue incorporates is decent comfortable seating. By having fitting seating where you and your family can fan out and appreciate sitting in front of the TV or films you will find that you are getting to know each other making the most of your venture than you would on the off chance that you discovered the seating solid and awkward. I likewise propose unique seating alternatives for more modest kids that permits them an exceptional spot to sit and no space for question over which seat has a place with whom. In addition to the fact that you want a decent comfortable spot for your little ones yet additionally a pleasant territory for the adults to appreciate and feel great also.

I energetically suggest that you additionally keep a pleasant inventory of nibble plate accessible for those occasions when the circumstance merits and numerous individuals incorporate smaller than expected ice chests and microwaves (for popcorn obviously) in their home auditorium so they don't need to travel far to appreciate some incredible rewards during ads or breaks in real life on the big screen.

While there is nobody size fits all home theater, there are numerous contacts you can add that will improve the auditorium experience in your home and make it considerably more agreeable for all included. Set aside the effort to choose what highlights you can add that will make the space turn out better for your requirements and that of your families film and TV watching inclinations and go with those contacts as opposed to attempting to adjust to a 'standard' that doesn't actually exist with regards to home theaters. The main thing you can do is make a space wherein you feel great watching motion pictures and TV as a family. In the event that you accomplish this specific objective you will have a home venue that is probably going to be the jealousy of others around you.

Beautifying your Home Theater on a Careful spending plan

In the event that you are sufficiently lucky to construct a room in your home that is committed to the motivation behind watching films or as a home theater it just bodes well that you might want to beautify the room in a way that is totally befitting of its motivation. There are stunning alternatives accessible inside this developing business sector of beautifying and by and large, there are costs that are intended to coordinate. Fortunately while craftsmanship regularly mirrors life, there is no explanation that we can't mimic a portion of the incredible workmanship we find in the motion pictures or on TVs shows in our homes—for a portion of the expense.

As a matter of first importance, a great home venue is a speculation, especially those that are for the most part utilized in private rooms. All things considered you will need to design your room in a way that won't divert from your film watching experience. There are numerous ways you can do this and a large number of them come at rather weighty expenses for the normal buyer. You don't need to buy uncommon lighting at $500 a pop when you can go to your neighborhood lighting or home improvement store and discover superb divider sconces that will be ideal for your home venue for a portion of the expense for which you will discover them at forte stores taking into account those structure home theaters. For all the more low lighting choices you can utilize modest strings of rope lighting or even Christmas tree lights to give some light without gambling a glare on the screen.

Maybe than balancing costly curtain on the dividers in your home theater you can apply finished paint in dull tones to try not to divert glares. Your neighborhood retailer may urge you to soundproof your dividers and you are the one in particular that can truly choose if that is vital. I for one would pass, especially if your home auditorium will be in a cellar, which is normally fairly eliminated from the remainder of your home and your family region.

To the extent flooring goes, hazier covering is a smart thought in many zones however potentially not the best in a storm cellar. Stopper makes a decent ground surface alternative for storm cellar floors as is attempts to mute sound from getting away from the room notwithstanding a characteristic protection from dampness related issues that may periodically emerge in a storm cellar. It is additionally an exceptionally cheap ground surface material that is profoundly misjudged.

I additionally suggest dim outfitting for your home theater. A decent decision may be obscurely shaded sectional couches on the off chance that you need the family to partake in the space together. I likewise suggest beanbags or other uncommon seating for the little ones who may make the most of your home auditorium too. This gives them their own seats and kills a portion of the quarreling and quarrels that frequently emerge over premium seating space.

The fact is that you don't need to spend a fortune to make an extraordinary environment that is absolutely helpful for a generally speaking lovely film watching experience in your home theater. While I don't suggest a lot of messiness along the dividers in this specific room you can do extraordinary things with plastic popcorn boxes and flameless tea light candles along the floor. Allow your creative mind to introduce imaginative choices to the expensive things you find in the niche stores you'll be astonished at a portion of the perfect things you think of.

Home Theater for Small Spaces

One explanation that numerous individuals who might cherish the advantages of a home performance center abstain from making the venture or in any event, considering their alternatives is on the grounds that they live in circumstances that permit almost no space with which to put the fundamental parts of a home theater framework. Fortunately minimal frameworks are filling in quality and accessibility as space all throughout the planet turns out to be increasingly restricted. As the populace develops, the issue of room develops also. Gone are the days loaded up with tremendous manor style homes all throughout the planet as networks are increasingly more regularly completely filled with high rises, apartment suites, and homes based on minimized parcels in lodging networks.

The normal family all throughout the planet has experience the restrictions of room with regards to things, for example, floor speakers and massive home theater frameworks. Fortunately they long stretches of colossal projectors and huge TVs stands have dropped off the radar to clear a path for roof mounted projectors and back projector TVs that fit firmly into corners when vital. We additionally have the additional accommodation of remote speakers that can be mounted on dividers or in the roof just as LCD and plasma TVs that can be mounted on the divider instead of taking up valuable land on our floors.

Space may have been a moderating element in the past with regards to the acquisition of a home theater however with the production of many box units and arising innovation it is not, at this point a substantial pardon not to push ahead into this hundred years of electronic accommodation and move quality picture and sound in the solace of your own special home. An ever increasing number of individuals are tracking down that a decent home auditorium is supplanting cash spent at theaters or games as they can get prevalent quality perspectives (and the comfort of moment replays) at home.

Regardless of whether you are one of numerous all throughout the planet who has put off this buy, which will significantly improve how you see home film seeing, there are choices that merit considering for your home theater needs with regards to the impediments of room. Regardless of whether you live in a loft that offers a minuscule living territory you can in any case appreciate extraordinary quality sound from a little home theater framework. These frameworks truth be told work preferable in little spaces over in rooms that are excessively enormous for them. Make certain to talk about your choices and what may be best for little spaces when you are tuning in to various frameworks and units in the store.

I think the main thing to remember when utilizing divider or roof mounted hardware in your home venue is that you may really find that you are opening up more space inside your room than would be busy with your present TV (this is particularly obvious in the event that you move up to a level TV that is mounted on the divider as opposed to a massive back projector TV or an immense amusement place.

In all actuality you never truly realize what is available and what will work in your space until you go out there and look at your choices. It is greatly improved to go out there and see what is accessible than deny yourself of the happiness a decent home performance center will bring dependent on a supposition that may not be valid for your home or condo.

Home Theater for the Little Ones

Your home performance center can be one room in which everybody loves to stare at the TV. Truth be told, in numerous homes it is the one room that is frequently utilized by the family. Nonetheless, clearly everybody inside a family doesn't generally concede to what is a proper film or TV decision at some random time. I know in my family father and child young lady regularly differ on whether Sunday football or one more survey of Cars, or whichever Disney flick makes them ceaseless consideration right now, has a higher review need.

In many examples father wins out as child young lady has practically limitless admittance to the TV while daddy is working during the week. Anyway a basic answer for this specific quandary is make a small home theater. Obviously then there will be battles among the little ones about who's turn it is, yet that is better compared to having them battle about seating position while you're attempting to watch a film or most loved network show (I think).

While some may imagine that the interest in a second home theater, particularly one for the children, is a fairly sizeable speculation, it can really be a serious wise venture no doubt. Above all else, the framework you buy for the children won't require best in class segments. This is one case where a container pack may be exactly what the circumstance calls for (and you can track down those sensibly estimated). Your little ones need neither a plasma TV nor a huge screen (they will in general sit a lot nearer to the sets than grown-ups so a more modest screen is better) and you could very well discover new parts to hold you over should something at any point go out on your home theater framework.

Something else to recall while choosing a home performance center for your kids is that they are not close to as requesting as grown-ups with regards to quality. Indeed, they will in any case be the jealousy of every one of their companions only by having speakers and encompass sound. They needn't bother with HD for one or the other picture or sound in their sets and Bose speakers while extraordinary are a smidgen of pointless excess for little ears that think the verses to Itsy-Bitsy Spider are persuasive.

Building a home theater framework for the children is additionally an incredible method to cause them to feel like they are critical to you. Most grown-ups truly appreciate (or disdain contingent upon how your group is getting along on some random Sunday) the time they share with their home theater. The way that you are giving something that carries you such a lot of delight with your little ones by giving them one to share is something incredible in their eyes and psyches. In all honesty, it will likewise show them obligation and to deal with things.

Consider the big picture, we frequently give our youngsters toys that are broken and disregarded in a simple matter of days. They see the consideration we take of our home theaters and are very likely (and as a rule shockingly) to follow our model. You can additionally delineate this by mentioning to them what should be done to appropriately focus on their home theater and help them to remember the results of inability to do as such (unlimited long stretches of football and no Disney) and they are regularly more than anxious to take great consideration of their unique home theater. Advise them that this is an extraordinary treat and they should regard it as that and you will be stunned at how compelling your words will be.

The harmony and calm that a second home venue can bring to your family is definitely worth the negligible speculation this framework ought to require. I can consider not many more prominent blessings you can give yourself as a grown-up than a couple of hours seven days of continuous congruity inside the family.

Home Theater Practicalities

The present customers are significantly more clever than they have been in days past. Maybe this complexity with regards to finding out about the items we spend our well deserved cash on is the aftereffect of moment data readily available through the Internet or a profound longing to find out about where our cash is going. Whatever the explanation, we are setting aside the effort to learn however much as could reasonably be expected about our ventures and cautiously arranging how we go through our cash before it leaves our wallets.

From numerous points of view this is magnificent information. You truly can't turn out badly as a purchaser my instructing yourself about the items you are thinking about buying and this holds doubly obvious with regards to gadgets. An ever increasing number of customers are opening up to home theaters. Indeed, this is turning into a selling point in numerous homes the nation over. It is an extraordinary thought to explore the items you will buy and the individual segments of your home theater framework however how long have you contributed towards the arranging and plan of your home theater?

You may have the room at the top of the priority list, however do you have the wiring you need? Are outlets in the right area to give the additional outlets you will require for your parts? Do you have the wiring for speakers set up or is this something extra you should consider? Will you go with remote speakers to stay away from the problem? There are such countless inquiries you should pose to yourself when making arrangements for your home theater.

What, of your current home amusement hardware will you keep and what bits of gear, assuming any, will you supplant? I generally suggest getting each part in turn and building a home theater framework as opposed to just going in and buying a case off the rack that has everything in one spot. While you can get a pleasant framework by doing this, I figure you will eventually get all the more value for your money on the off chance that you fabricate your own framework each piece in turn and select each piece for the individual characteristics your like. That being said, when you get the segments home you should have the option to introduce them and join them into your current home theater.

Will you add exceptional home performance center seating or going with a major comfortable sofa? This issue when arranging the design for the room wherein you will watch your motion pictures and TV top picks. You need the seating to be agreeable or nobody will need to invest too horrendously much energy in the room, regardless of how enormous the TV screen is. We like to be agreeable as we watch 24 hours of relentless activity or the closest planet in a distant nearby planetary group detonate. Do you have an arrangement for giving that solace in your home theater?

Do you have the entirety of the associating wires? What about a dependable strategy for masking the wires so they don't give an interruption during your film and TV seeing time? It is safe to say that you will add gaming hardware to your home theater framework? Assuming this is the case, this opens up a whole new ball game with regards to wires, as you will bring considerably more lines and wires and regulators in with the general mish-mash.

The following inquiry is how would you intend to conceal all the hardware? While worked in amusement places may appear to be an extraordinary thought, they are executioners to your primary concern should you need to some time or another sell your home as they gobble up floor space and not every person will see the value in your home theater. Therefore, I prescribe a story to-roof diversion focus with entryways that can be shut around the highlights you're not utilizing out of the blue.

While there is no correct with regards to planning a home performance center for your family, there are down to earth matters that are certainly worth considering. I trust this has inferred a couple of those and that you are overflowing with awesome thoughts for your current or future home theater.

Home Theater Speaker Basics

Quite possibly the most fundamental parts of a decent home venue is its speakers. You essentially can't accomplish that theater climate in the event that you don't have great speakers from which to appreciate the sound that is a particularly fundamental piece of a decent 'film going' experience. The issue is that a great many people are effortlessly befuddled with respect to which speakers they truly need for their home theater setups just as the legitimate arrangement of those speakers to make a genuine encompass sound.

Coming up next are the essential speakers that are needed to finish a decent home theater: front left and right speakers, a middle channel speaker, encompass sound speakers, and subwoofers. Focus channel speakers are ignored and avoided with regards to many home theaters. I advise against doing as such as these speakers supply a decent part of the soundtrack in numerous motion pictures just as add completion and profundity to the discourse.

Encompass sound speakers are what give the foundation sounds that cause the motion pictures to appear to be all the more genuine. These are the things that bring watchers into films and add a smidgen of fervor to the way toward watching a film. All things considered, they are vital to remember for your home theater, as they will help match the performance center insight. Basic alternatives for encompass sound speakers incorporate 5.1 channel, 6.1 channel, or 7.1 channel encompass.

Subwoofers are liable for the profound bass sound that lines so numerous film soundtracks. These sounds are liable for making feeling and show inside the soundtrack and are great at setting up anticipation and different feelings that are a significant part in the film insight. A decent arrangement of subwoofers is fundamental in your home theater speaker bundle or you will pass up a decent arrangement of the adrenaline that is made because of sound in theaters.

While there are numerous brands from which to pick it is significant that you pick speakers that will function admirably together by making a comparative sound. The most ideal choice for this is to buy all speakers together in one pack by one producer. It could be enticing to save assets to blend and match speakers yet this won't make the genuine nature of sound you are wanting to accomplish in your home theater.

Notwithstanding the numerous brands of speakers for your home theater you may likewise find that there are additionally a wide range of styles of speakers. There are those that sit on shelves, satellite speakers, and floor speakers. Floor speakers much of the time give the best solid. On the disadvantage they additionally take up the most land inside your room which can be genuinely restricting and make them an ugly choice for some. You even had the special reward of remote speakers arising in quality and limit.

There is no set in stone with regards to speakers for your home theater. They will have an immense effect on the general auditorium influence of your framework however like each and every other segment the speakers are as yet a matter of taste. A few group lean toward watching films at home since they can handle the volume and don't feel the tension and, for example, essentially as they do in theaters. For those you might need to bring down the volume for your encompass speakers or your subwoofers. Notwithstanding, the essential target is to make a home theater you can appreciate and legitimate speakers contribute extraordinarily to that pleasure.

Recognizing your Home Theater Needs

On the off chance that you are on the lookout for a home theater framework, odds are that you have a very smart thought of the individual segments you will require to make your framework complete. The vast majority discover questions with regards to explicit data about the individual pieces and parts of the framework. Nonetheless, with an end goal to teach about home theater frameworks, this will be a short separate of parts that one may hope to buy throughout building a superior home theater framework. Remember that everybody will have their own particular necessities and inclinations and you may have some totally adequate segments as of now. This obviously, will get a good deal on the general buy in the event that you decide to keep the pieces you right now own.

As a matter of first importance, there are a wide range of 'home auditorium in a crate' packs available today. These units are as of now set up to assist you with getting the home theater you want all at once. While you can get totally great home theater frameworks thusly, I genuinely trust you will improve an incentive for your cash by building your own framework each segment in turn. On the off chance that you are restless in a rush or essentially don't wish to invest the energy investigating your alternatives then the home theater frameworks that are sold available might be a smart thought for you.

Since we've moved beyond that, you should see that a few group believe the real TV to be a piece of the home theater framework. You can go numerous courses while choosing a TV that will work with your home theater needs. It is completely dependent upon you what sort of TV you select. I do anyway suggest that you truly think about the lighting in some random room prior to picking your TV. Projection TVs don't do well in rooms with a lot of light. Something else, go with what works inside your financial plan and the general look you like for your home auditorium seeing.

Sound is another significant part of most home theater frameworks. The sum you spend on your sound framework ought to rely altogether upon how much solid effects your satisfaction in films. You can spend a great deal of cash on a decent arrangement of speakers and sound framework or you can truly reduce expenses by saving on this specific segment. Everything with regards to building a home auditorium relies totally on your own inclinations and the general framework you wish to fabricate.

To get the best profit by your speakers you will require a beneficiary to deal with the sounds and present them in the most ideal light. The beneficiary fundamentally gets data from all way of gadgets and conveys the message where you advise it to go. Your recipient is one spot that a great many people will in general spend a decent bit of their financial plan and in light of current circumstances. This is by a wide margin perhaps the main segments and one that numerous individuals don't effectively possess.

Your DVD/DVR is something else that can affect your survey insight. You shouldn't select a superior quality DVD or DVR except if you have a top quality TV and really at that time in the event that you intend to buy superior quality DVDs as opposed to the standard DVDs you will discover available right now. Doing so will just bring about a misuse of cash while the innovation is new. All things considered, stand by a little while until the costs drop and overhaul gradually instead of purchasing the best in class most costly part that the rest of your framework can't stay aware of.

While this rundown is in no way, shape or form thorough of all that you may wish to remember for your home theater framework it will give a decent beginning to most home theaters. No one but you can set your financial plan and choose the amount you will spend on every individual segment. My best counsel is to begin with a beneficiary and construct your framework each part in turn around your collector.

Media Center Driven Home Theaters

The present PCs are being called upon to accomplish more different errands than at some other point ever. Truth be told, the utilization of PCs as a fundamental piece of a home auditorium is getting increasingly more typical as innovation advances. There are in any event, working frameworks planned upon the possibility of a PC being utilized as an overall media focus as opposed to simply working as a PC.

Subsequently, I see the development in this treatment and utilization of PCs filling in fame just as probability later on. With an ever increasing number of individuals consolidating their PC use into different parts of work and play it just bodes well that we presently bring them above and beyond in their diversion capacities and abilities. The innovation anyway isn't totally new, what's happening is the developing number of individuals putting this innovation to use on a normal, if not regular schedule.

Media Center PCs are PCs that basically act in the limit that a collector would typically act. They acknowledge the data and send it where it ought to go. These PCs permit you to tune in to music through the speakers on the PC or through those that are essential for your home sound system just as DVDs, mp3s, and so on You can likewise utilize these frameworks to stare at the TV programs on your PC screen instead of a TV. This implies you can likewise utilize your PC hard drive to store advanced accounts of your #1 TV program. Notwithstanding these incredible highlights, you can likewise make slideshows with your advanced photos.

While a couple of years prior you would have been taunted for the thought that your home PC would demonstrate an important asset for your home theater, the utilization is getting increasingly more generally acknowledged and rehearses. We will just consider more prominent to be of this happening as innovation develops and advances to a point where PCs may one day become a fundamental segment in any great quality home theater framework that is sold on any market.

By taking the time currently to figure out how to utilize this innovation for your potential benefit you are making way for significantly more noteworthy things to come later on for your home theater framework and to expand your own happiness regarding the space that is your home theater. As innovation propels we will see upgrades of usefulness of media focus PCs just as approaches to extend their present limit and carry more highlights to them. For the present, they offer the best mix of capacity and diversion I have encountered inside my lifetime. I'm anticipating see the things on the way with media focus PCs and the mix of home theater innovation with the effectiveness and control that PCs permit in with the general mish-mash.

In the event that you have not yet thought to be the extra profundity that joining your PC with your home venue can give there is no time better compared to the president to look at how it can help your and your present setup. While you are busy you may likewise wish to look at propels that are being made on the two fronts and how they supplement each other while thinking about future buys or redesigns for your present home theater.

Exploring every available opportunity with Home Theater Systems

On the off chance that you are on the lookout for a home theater framework chances are you are encountering some level of shell stun at all the choices that are accessible in the present market. The way that there are such countless alternatives is both great and appalling simultaneously. The sheer measure of rivalry is functioning admirably to drive costs down for purchasers. In light of that, there are still degrees of evaluating as per the nature of home theater framework you are choosing. Then again, an immense amount of determination for some, settles on narrowing down the appropriate decision for explicit necessities troublesome, best case scenario.

There are a few things to remember when buying a home theater framework and the first of those things is to choose a financial plan and stick with it. The actual interaction of building up a spending limits your choices and you just might be amazed at the quality you can discover inside different financial plans. Much more astounding to numerous shoppers is the way that you don't need to go with names that you know to get brilliant nature of sound, picture, and worth from your home theater framework.

I energetically suggest that you see every framework in real life that you are thinking about prior to settling on one. I additionally profoundly propose that you never let cost alone be the central consideration of which home theater framework you buy. On the off chance that you can't manage the cost of the situation you need right currently put something aside for one more little while to buy the framework that you genuinely feel will be the best incentive for your cash and your home. You will spend numerous hours, on the off chance that you are a run of the mill American, making the most of your home theater framework, it just bodes well that you will cause a genuine interest in getting the quality you to merit from your framework. In the event that you don't choose a framework that is acceptable quality you will just wind up spending more by supplanting it sooner than needed over the long haul.

The following best idea I can make when you are choosing the appropriate home theater framework for you and your family is to make a rundown of needs with regards to highlights. In the event that you as of now have an amazing quality DVD player it looks bad to pay extra for a home auditorium that incorporates a DVD player, especially if that player would be of substandard quality. Do you require great quality sound or is the sound of minor significance to you? There are a wide range of spots you can reduce expenses when buying a home theater framework and the vast majority of them are only matters of taste, inclination, and need.

Understanding what you need when you start your quest for a home theater setup is by a long shot the most ideal approach to try not to purchase a framework that is mismatched for your home or your requirements. In the event that you have hearing issues and need a bunch of earphones to hear the TV all things considered, a costly strong framework is squandered cash similar to your own requirements. In the event that you are utilizing a sunroom for your home theater or a room that is splendidly lit, a projection TV would be basically pointless for your requirements. You should bend over backward not to go through cash where cash isn't required and save your first-class buys for things that will mean the most to your framework.

Another significant thing to recall when looking and contrasting home auditoriums is that you don't need to make the whole buy all at once. It is entirely conceivable to buy each piece in turn to take full advantage of your cash and really appreciate each redesigned part as it enhances your current home theater. Getting each piece in turn likewise assists you with narrowing down ensuing buys by realizing what highlights are required notwithstanding the things that you right now have. The main recommendation I can give you is this: the motivation behind your home theater framework is to keep you engaged so you are the only one it needs to intrigue.

Appropriate Lighting Makes Home Theater Systems

The most ideal area for the normal home venue would be a cellar room that permits almost no or no regular daylight to sneak into the room. There are so numerous things you can do in a cellar that just strengthen the venue experience of your normal home theater. From real arena or theater seating to rope lights that line the side of the dividers (where it meets the floor) for low encompassing lighting that won't divert from the screen or bring about any superfluous glare. Out of the numerous things you can decide to upgrade your home theater, lighting may really be quite possibly the most significant just as the frequently neglected.

In the event that you are sufficiently lucky to have a storm cellar, this is an ideal area for a home auditorium however don't surrender on the off chance that you live in an environment that isn't by and large helpful for home storm cellars. Indeed, even in the daylight cellar there are steps you can take to keep a lot of light from influencing your home venue experience. Some smart thoughts with which to begin is buy dark out shades that keep daylight from crawling into your room. This looks far superior to the antiquated handy solution of setting aluminum foil over your windows without a doubt.

Indeed, even inside your room in the event that you've set aside the effort to ensure characteristic light isn't sneaking in you may find that inadequately positioned lighting antagonistically influences your review delight. When introducing your home theater framework you need to give cautious consideration to both normal and fake light at various occasions of day to perceive what they mean for your capacity to see the TV (this is especially significant on the off chance that you have a projection TV) just as to check whether there is any glare on your TV screen from light looking through your window ornaments or from lights and overhead lighting inside the room.

Recessed lighting is a decent choice for most home auditorium rooms as is rope lighting as I referenced previously. In the event that you have this kind of lighting you can see alright to move around without hindering what is occurring on your TV screen. Furthermore, low lighting in the room causes the real TV to turn into the point of convergence of the room at whatever point it is on and the overhead lights are down.

On the off chance that you are making a home venue themed room you may discover a portion of the fascinating film time divider sconces of extraordinary interest. These sconces lean toward low degrees of light that are probably not going to meddle extraordinarily with what's going on your TV screen. You can discover a wide range of superb sconces in a wide assortment of subjects. It bodes well that with home performance center lighting assuming a particularly vital part in the general delight in the home auditorium experience that numerous organizations are being made just to fill this need inside the lighting business.

Some will contend that the TV you decide for your home auditorium is uncontrollably more significant than the lighting in the room by a long shot. I will in general clash. In the event that you don't take care to guarantee that the lighting in the room isn't suitable it is impossible that you will actually want to completely appreciate the TV you chose. Thus I generally figure you should save your present TV for some time, test it out with the lighting and put resources into appropriate lighting prior to making an interest in a greater or better TV to add to your home theater framework.

Everything with regards to a home auditorium are comparative with individual inclination just like everything throughout everyday life. Set aside the effort to truly consider the influence that the lighting in the room that will turn into your home performance center will influence your capacity to see the motion pictures or network shows that you appreciate to such an extent. When you have the ideal circumstance with regards to lighting you will be flabbergasted at the amount more you really make the most of your home theater.

Legitimate Seating Key to Home Theater Enjoyment

There are a great deal of things that go into making the ideal home performance center that numerous individuals may never consider when buying singular segments, pieces, and parts. A decent home auditorium is substantially more than a spot to proceed to sit in front of the TV around evening time; it is a film and TV seeing experience. You need to ensure that you are making a room that isn't only agreeable for a couple of individuals yet for everybody that will appreciate the chance to see motion pictures, movies, or TV in this room.

One approach to guarantee that everybody will be agreeable and effectively ready to see the screen and therefore appreciate the experience you will likewise need to give close consideration to the seating you decide for your home theater. There are various seating alternatives for the normal home theater framework. The absolute generally famous right now is the thing that is viewed as the 'theater chair'. Indeed, many home theater sweethearts incline toward watching films at home for the solace of the seating alone. I do anyway prescribe including choices for individuals to rest (my main objection with regards to going to genuine theaters). Most theater chairs permit this choice.

The theater chair is interesting to numerous on the grounds that it has armrests for every individual and a spot to hold your beverages. You don't need to set tables in the middle, the seats can be arranged close to each other and you can appreciate every others organization while watching your #1 film or TV program. There is in no way like appreciating the theater air in the solace of your home.

Notwithstanding the theater chair, in the event that you need a more retro feel in your home theater or to set up 'bistro' tables you can pick lounger seats in your home theater. This is incredible in the event that you intend to have a ton of pizza night film encounters or have little youngsters that need a table to eat and sit in front of the TV or motion pictures or even to appreciate other calm exercises while you are getting a charge out of motion pictures and TV. It's an incredible method to bring a pleasant family feel to your home theater.

On the off chance that the seating types above are definitely not interesting to your sensibilities you very well could find that there is no spot like home for watching films and nothing more agreeable than a huge comfortable sofa. I for one love the solace of a major delicate couch with warm snuggly covers, particularly in the wintertime for appreciating films. It's an incredible route for the children to accumulate together and appreciate genuine nestle time while watching the most recent Disney flick or even Saturday morning kid's shows. Who needs to contribute a little fortune on a home auditorium that isn't utilized for regular survey at any rate?

In the event that you need to make your home auditorium particularly kid amicable you can select some crazy furniture for your little ones to appreciate. This will keep everybody cheerful, nobody battling for a most loved seat, and a substantially more serene film seeing experience for what it's worth. In the event that you need to be the coolest parent on the square you can incorporate a few additional items of this stylish uncommon child furniture for those occasions when guests are available.

There are numerous things associated with building the ideal home theater framework for you and your family. Making the ideal agreeable air in which to make the most of your auditorium is an extraordinary method to make this room the regularly utilized room in the house and unite the family every single night for some different option from supper. On the off chance that you need to encounter much more from your home performance center seating make certain to incorporate capacity for pads and covers close within reach for those evenings when some additional glow or a cushion to take cover behind is exactly what the circumstance merits. Have some good times evaluating the numerous choices for home performance center seating and pick the seats that you feel will turn out best for your family.

Choosing the Proper Television for your Home Theater

While there are a huge number that make up the normal home theater framework a great many people regularly disregard the significance of their TVs to the general video and film watching experience. Similarly as with everything throughout everyday life, greater, with regards to TVs for your home theater, isn't in every case better. There are numerous things that should be viewed as while choosing the most ideal TV for your home theater and size is just one of many.

Mass retailers show TVs in a way that suits their motivation, which is a deal. This doesn't imply that their techniques for showing their TVs paints those sets in a legitimate light for your home survey insight. In the no so distant past, a 20-inch seeing window for your TV was considered enormous. It was an extravagance put something aside for the individuals who were incredibly well off. The reality of the situation is that in the event that you don't sit an appropriate separation from your TV the nature of the image will look appalling if your set is excessively huge.

There are acceptable dependable guidelines to consider when buying a TV for your room, at any rate where size is concerned. The standard is that you will need close to 4" of slanting screen crawls on your TV for each foot away from the set you will be when watching digital TV. The standard goes up to 5 inches for each foot for satellite TV or DVDs, and 6 inches for every foot on the off chance that you are seeing superior quality TV.

Obviously with each standard there are exemptions. For this standard general exemptions would be two story extraordinary rooms or basilica roofs that may really require a bigger TV and cellars or dropped roofs that may real be more qualified for more modest TVs. You truly should think about these things while choosing the TV that will best suit your necessities with regards to your home theater and your performance center set up.

Obviously there is more than size to consider with regards to the TV you eventually decide for your home theater and taste just as space will each assume significant parts in the TV you ought to pick. One significant thought is cost. At the point when you stroll into the store and see every one of the great new TVs that guarantee unlimited long periods of film watching rapture at a powerful sticker price to coordinate. You should have the option to filter out without getting diverted by the best in class of extravagant accessories to track down the set that will meet the entirety of your film observing necessities and fall inside your spending plan.

For this specific excursion I suggest strolling in with cash close by (the breaking point you have set) and that you leave the Visa at home. You ought to likewise cautiously consider whether you will need a service agreement as that will raise the base cost of your TV and isn't reflected in the 'retail cost. In the event that you bring your charge card you will be enticed to overspend as opposed to staying with your unique financial plan.

Other than value you truly need to painstakingly consider the kind of TV you'd prefer to have for your home theater. Remember that you can purchase bigger renditions of more established innovation at a similar cost you'd pay for more modest screen sizes with regards to LCD TVs. You ought to likewise consider the size of the TV you truly need for this segment as well. The vast majority of us don't sit in excess of 12 feet from our TVs, which implies you may not need very as much TV as you may have recently figured you would require. The main thing while picking a TV is to recollect that this is a venture that the majority of us don't make frightfully regularly. Hence you ought to hope to drop a significant wad of cash on this specific interest in your home theater framework.

The Great Installation Debate

One enormous inquiries looms in the personalities of numerous who choose for buy gigantic home theater frameworks for their homes: Do I introduce it myself or pay for establishment? This extraordinary discussion appears to devour customers the world over and there truly is no simple answer as it totally and completely relies upon your own certainty of your capacities and whether you will defer the labor for a half year or get right to it once you get your home theater—well home.

In my home everything relies upon who needs the item most and who can deal with an establishment. I've discovered that with regards to things, for example, home performance centers my significant other is a pro at completing it properly away. Then again I hauled my clothing to the clothing mat for about a month and a half while a clothes washer and dryer sat in my cellar hanging tight for him to introduce them. In view of this, I pay for establishment on anything that I need introduced rapidly and in the event that it doesn't make any difference excessively appallingly a lot to me, I'll leave it to him to introduce on his own timetable.

Obviously timing isn't the solitary thought with regards to the establishment of your home theater gear. Information is really a key part. In the event that you break something over the span of establishment it may not be covered by the guarantee, especially in the event that it is not difficult to demonstrate that it was broken and not the aftereffect of a manufacturing plant deformity. Simultaneously you don't wish to get down to the last tad just to find that one little part is missing, which may really expect you to take everything out, take care of it, and return it to the store. Time is cash for a significant number of us and going through the establishment cycle twice isn't just disappointing it is costly (even as far as the measure of our recreation time it denies us of).

There are obviously different contemplations with regards to the choice of whether to address the cost of expert establishment and one of those is the guarantee on your home theater framework and its parts. There are a few guarantees that are invalidated in the event that you don't have your home theater plant or expertly introduced. You should be sure in the event that you are introducing your own home venue that your guarantee will not be squandered subsequently.

There are positives to consider with regards to introducing your home venue also. Number one on that rundown is the measure of cash you will save. Proficient establishment (anything with proficient before it besides) is very exorbitant and numerous buyers disregard to consider that while planning for their home theaters. Much of the time proficient establishment can be a genuine article breaker with regards to getting the home theater framework that you truly need.

The second sure with regards to playing out the establishment yourself is that you know unquestionably how to dismantle it and move the pieces in the event that you at any point have the event or need to do as such (like a move or the need to fix or supplant certain pieces or parts). It is likewise a smart thought to realize where everything connects and doing the establishment yourself will give you an obvious sign of that also.

At long last, there is a feeling of pride that accompanies realizing you did it without anyone else's help and you did it well. Having the option to achieve something that not every person is capable or able to do all alone is noteworthy and something you should invest wholeheartedly in doing. Regardless of whether you choose to go with proficient establishment (there is no disgrace in this choice) or introducing your home theater framework for yourself I wish you numerous long stretches of happiness with your new home theater.

Why Buy Home Theater Kits?

You will discover a wide range of homes around the country and all throughout the planet. Some are huge, some are little, and some are just normal. At the point when you are looking for home theater frameworks you will track down exactly the same thing. This is especially valid for the home theater frameworks that come as a bundle bargain. While I don't ordinarily support these buys, similarly as all homes are not the same, nor are for the most part individuals. This implies that what might be best for me and my home performance center may not be the best strategy for you and your home theater.

I certainly prescribe tuning in to any home theater you are thinking about prior to diving in and buying. There are commonly in life when you get what you pay for. While the vast majority of us live inside some level of spending requirements you will track down that a large portion of us have certain things we essentially won't go 'modest' when buying. You should remember that there are extraordinary approaches to get remarkable deals in any case, with regards to buying hardware. One of these ways is by buying a home venue pack where every one of the pieces (for the most part except for the TV) are incorporated.

Truth can be stranger than fiction with regards to an incentive for a large portion of us. The most ideal approach to track down a home venue pack that you will be certain about buying is to investigate the unit, tune in to the speakers (the initial 5 to 10 minutes of the film Top Gun is a magnificent test for sound), and investigate the framework to perceive how you discover the interface. It doesn't make any difference how extraordinary a framework sounds on the off chance that you can't sort out some way to utilize it whenever you've removed it from the case. You may likewise need to investigate the cost of expert establishment in the event that you are electronically tested with regards to issue of programming and establishment. These packs are additionally frequently interesting to the individuals who discover the possibility of looking for the parts and segments drawn-out.

While it is hard for me to acknowledge on occasion, we were not all conceived customers. For individuals, for example, this, home theater frameworks that come as a bundle bargain are frequently life rings threw out in an ocean of shopping among sharks. This accommodation at some merits any cost that could be stepped on the case. Fortunately there is sufficient contest that costs are ordinarily aggressive as indicated by quality.

Box pack home theater frameworks are interesting to numerous purchasers for a wide range of reasons. The individuals who live in little condos or have minuscule home venue rooms commonly find that it looks bad to put resources into a framework that will shake the dividers or have the neighbors grumbling. Those with restricted spending plans track down that this is a monetary method to get everything simultaneously. Individuals who have brief period to put resources into exploring every one of the things they will require discover it unfathomably helpful that they won't have to stress over missing something significant like a collector during the interaction. Still others find that they like knowing in advance what the cost for the absolute home auditorium experience will be, in any event the gadgets part at any rate.

Recall that a home auditorium implies various things to various individuals. Tracking down the ideal home auditorium for you may not really liken to the ideal home venue for another person who has great dreams of a film themed room with dull rich tones on the dividers and quieted lighting impacts alongside passed out windows for a definitive film seeing experience.

Try not to get too gotten up to speed in the subtleties and recollect that it just needs to work for you and your requirements. Making a brilliant home auditorium is an extraordinary method to unite the family consistently. Purchasing a pre made home venue pack or framework is an incredible method to start appreciating the magnificent advantages of a home auditorium experience while learning the things you like and aversion about your framework. This could be a work in progress for a long time to come as you get familiar with what you do a lot not like.

Remote Speakers Offer Excellent Sound Selection

Innovation is continually developing and acquainting new items with a generally full line of home theater items. While not the most up to date kids on the square, remote speaker innovation is additionally progressing at a rate that costs are not, at this point far from the normal customer and the benefit of having the option to move your speakers around without going to crafted by reworking is interesting to shoppers on an undeniably enormous scope.

I generally attempt to remember when purchasing new gadgets and electronic parts that the current year's innovation will sell at a large portion of the value this time one year from now. Therefore I struggle putting resources into the best in class with regards to innovation and will in general remain precisely one age disappointing when purchasing new items. I like to set aside cash at whatever point conceivable and as a rule my like of setting aside cash exceeds my like of having new devices and thingamabobs at the excessive cost they regularly order.

I additionally have an awful propensity for keeping those items until they are not, at this point valuable by any means (I actually have my little 13 inch TV from my school quarters and I will not reveal to you how quite a while in the past that was). I will keep it until it does not work anymore. It is as of now being utilized in my TV. I just notice this to pass on the way that making a sizeable interest in gadgets as a rule is a speculation that will keep going for a long while except if you are one of those individuals who must have the best in class new tech toy every single year.

Back to my unique point remote speakers have been arising innovation for a couple of years at this point. We've at long last grown sufficient contest that market costs are moving downwards. This makes now the ideal opportunity to investigate the choice of buying remote speakers for your home theater. They are as yet a sizeable venture for the normal home theater customer however definitely justified as I would like to think for the opportunity of decision and development that they give.

This is an incredible extra in the event that you have a current home performance center set up and are thinking about an overhaul. I feel that numerous individuals will track down that the alternatives this bears the cost of makes it certainly worth the speculation that will be needed to accomplish. I firmly suggest anyway that you don't just go on the web and purchase the main arrangement of remote speakers and beneficiary that you find. This is a genuine bet, as you have no clue about what sort of value you will get. The most ideal suggestion is to get out and about of neighborhood stores and tune in to the different frameworks that are available.

Whenever you've tracked down the one remote sound framework that advances most to you the time has come to go online to analyze costs. Whenever you've tracked down the best cost online you should then check your nearby stores and check whether they offer a low cost gurantee that will coordinate with the online value you found. This is an incredible method to discover more ideal arrangements and set aside a little cash (by not paying delivery charges).

You ought to consistently remember that there are no absolutes with regards to making a home theater. You don't need to follow a particular code, or utilize certain segments or even certain seating. Everything thing you can manage is to make a climate wherein you and your family can best make the most of your TV and film seeing encounters. You should remember the sounds you like while choosing speakers and pick speakers that will give the fullest measure of sound that you are alright with paying your well deserved cash to buy. Truly, this is your cash and your home performance center is a venture you should take extraordinary consideration to make the most ideal speculation for your cash.

Don't miss out!

Visit the website below and you can sign up to receive emails whenever Jim Stephens publishes a new book. There's no charge and no obligation.

https://books2read.com/r/B-A-VNEK-UMQPB

BOOKS 2 READ

Connecting independent readers to independent writers.

Also by Jim Stephens

Kindle Publishing Made Easy: Autopilot Cash With Amazon Kindle!
Million-Dollar Secrets of the Amazon Associates: How They Make Money
From the Biggest Online Shopping Mall
Self-Publishing Made Easy: The Easy Way to Self-publish Your Own Books!
Scam Busters: How to Avoid the Most Popular Scams of Today!
Affiliate Marketing and Blogging
The Quick and Easy Guide of Diamonds
Government Information
Hiking and Camping
Home Theater Systems

About the Publisher

Accepting manuscripts in the most categories. We love to help people get their words available to the world.

Revival Waves of Glory focus is to provide more options to be published. We do traditional paperbacks, hardcovers, audio books and ebooks all over the world. A traditional royalty-based publisher that offers self-publishing options, Revival Waves provides a very author friendly and transparent publishing process, with President Bill Vincent involved in the full process of your book. Send us your manuscript and we will contact you as soon as possible.

Contact: Bill Vincent at rwgpublishing@yahoo.com www.rwgpublishing.com